THE CRAZY WORLD OF
GARDENING

CARTOONS BY

Bilstarr

■ EXLEY
NEW YORK · WATFORD, UK

Other cartoon giftbooks in this series:
The Crazy World of Cats (Bill Stott)
The Crazy World of Football (Bill Stott)
The Crazy World of Golf (Mike Scott)
The Crazy World of Housework (Bill Stott)
The Crazy World of Marriage (Bill Stott)
The Crazy World of Rugby (Bill Stott)
The Crazy World of Sex (Bill Stott)

First published in hardback in the USA in 1996 by Exley Giftbooks.
Published in Great Britain in 1996 by Exley Publications Ltd.

12   11   10   9   8   7   6   5   4

Copyright © Bill Stott, 1987

ISBN 1-85015-765-0

Printed in China.

Exley Publications Ltd., 16 Chalk Hill, Watford, Herts, WD1 4BN, United Kingdom.
Exley Publications LLC, 232 Madison Avenue, Suite 1409, NY 10016, USA.

"OK you bugs and beetles, weeds and weevils, remember me from last year? Well, I'm back!"

"Grandma's been stung again, Daddy..."

"When your mother remodels the garden,
she doesn't mess around"

"One of these days I'm going to buy an extension cable
and find out how much land I really have..."

"Steve reckons there's this one particular slug..."

"No. I think it was better where we had it in the first place..."

"Quick! Turn off the water and bring me a knife!"

"You've decided to tackle the old vegetable patch then?"

"So I said to George, 'We've got the land, we've got the money – let's have a <u>real</u> rock garden!'"

"Ah, here it is... 'Sometimes called Throttleweed from the legend of it being responsible for the disappearance of at least one of Henry VIII's gardeners...'"

"And that's where I fell off the steps..."

"Would it hurt so much to clean the bathroom when you've finished?"

"Working hard, my foot! He's been having a smoke behind the shed!"

"I take it back! I take it back! Your fingers are greener
than mine..."

"...and technically speaking, it's yours!"

"I'm signing him on for Pyromaniacs Anonymous next week..."

"That's Mrs Fisher. She has a sticking throttle..."

"I suppose you don't have a deodorized version, do you?"

"You let him go in there <u>alone</u>?!?"

"And your little friends dropped by to help you clean out the shed, did they? How nice!"

"Hello dear! Cousin George dropped by; he's out on the lawn
practising his chip shots..."

"Hi sweetheart, I'm home early. Come and meet our new Head of Sales..."

"I'm worried about your dad. He's always *talked* to his plants, but just recently he's started to listen to them as well!"

"It <u>is</u> the cat! About 10 minutes ago I spilled some of this new fertilizer on it..."

"David can get very emotional when he's thinning out the raspberry canes..."

"OK, here they come. You wriggle around,
and I'll run up his leg..."

"Honey? Have you seen my blue pin-stripe suit –
the one you don't like...?"

"It's a tribute to my husband's contribution to this garden..."

"Buzz off!"

"There now – be brave! Real gardeners don't cry when they
stick the pitchfork through their foot..."

"I didn't have the heart to tell him face to face..."

"I've been reconsidering. Don't you think pools are getting rather common? Why don't we have a nice rock garden instead?"

"Let's see the Jones's beat that!"

"No this is 28 Fairdrive Hill. You want 28 Fairhill Drive..."

"Bearing in mind the widely-held theory that plants respond and flourish when praised, I'm off to insult a few weeds..."

"Daddy's found a big worm? Well, good for him!"

"Evicting him seems a little heartless. After all, you only discovered him because you decided to clean up this section."

"Dandelion colony, bearing 020, behind the hollyhocks..."

"It's a new rose I've developed. It needs a lot of propping up;
I'm thinking of naming it after you."

"We're not speaking. I inadvertently disturbed the gerbil's last resting place while planting out the lettuce!"

"Strange how the mere mention of trimming the hedge gives
your back spasms..."

"The lucky horseshoe fell off the garage wall onto my head.
I staggered forward, put the mower into 'drive' inadvertently,
thereby destroying the fence. Then it overheated, burst into
flames, and really ruined my day!"

"C'mon son, don't be chicken! I bet I can dig up more seedlings than you can before he spots us..."

"I don't seem to be able to switch it off..."

"That's funny. There's a sand wedge and two old putters missing ..."

"That's weird. I moved my chair and the hose-pipe dried up..."

"She hates killing things. She thinks there's a slim chance of insulting the slugs out of the garden."

"Why not eat all of *one* leaf, instead of nibbling them all?"

"Stop moaning Gloria! I'm not paying good money for a summerhouse and then not use it!"

"What do you expect from a seed called 'Pot Luck'?"

"Of course, the pressure needs a little fine-tuning..."

"You're quite right Sir! It doesn't say anything about
having to wear gloves..."

"Yes, those little blue berries are poisonous!"

"Wouldn't it be easier just to learn their names?"

Books in the "Crazy World" series

The Crazy World of Cats (Bill Stott)
The Crazy World of Football (Bill Stott)
The Crazy World of Gardening (Bill Stott)
The Crazy World of Golf (Mike Scott)
The Crazy World of Housework (Bill Stott)
The Crazy World of Marriage (Bill Stott)
The Crazy World of Rugby (Bill Stott)
The Crazy World of Sex (Bill Stott)

Books in the "Fanatic's" series

The Fanatic's Guides are perfect presents for
everyone with a hobby that has got out of hand.
Over fifty hilarious colour cartoons by Roland Fiddy.

The Fanatic's Guide to Cats
The Fanatic's Guide to Computers
The Fanatic's Guide to Dads
The Fanatic's Guide to D.I.Y.
The Fanatic's Guide to Golf
The Fanatic's Guide to Husbands
The Fanatic's Guide to Love
The Fanatic's Guide to Sex

Great Britain: Order these super books from
your local bookseller or from Exley Publications Ltd,
16 Chalk Hill, Watford, Herts WDI 4BN.
(Please send £1.30 to cover postage and packing
on 1 book, £2.60 on 2 or more books.)